Jenny
Godwin

TIME TO CONSIDER

TIME TO CONSIDER

SELECTED POEMS BY
Mildred Cousens

Introduction by Philip Booth

1989
WILLIAM L. BAUHAN, PUBLISHER
DUBLIN, NEW HAMPSHIRE

COPYRIGHT © 1989 BY MILDRED COUSENS
INTRODUCTION COPYRIGHT © 1989 BY PHILIP BOOTH
ALL RIGHTS RESERVED

LIBRARY OF CONGRESS CATALOGUING IN PUBLICATION DATA:

COUSENS, MILDRED, 1904–
TIME TO CONSIDER: SELECTED POEMS / BY MILDRED COUSENS:
INTRODUCTION BY PHILIP BOOTH.
P.   CM.
ISBN 0-87233-099-0
I. TITLE
PS3553.0864T56   1989
811'.54—DC20   89-15016

PRINTED IN THE UNITED STATES OF AMERICA.
THIS BOOK WAS TYPESET IN LINOTRON BEMBO BY TCI, CHICOPEE, MASS., PRINTED BY
D&E GRAPHICS, INC., FITCHBURG, MASS., AND BOUND AT THE NEW HAMPSHIRE
BINDERY, CONCORD, N.H. DESIGNED BY W.L. BAUHAN

For *Ted* and *Teddy*
then and now

Acknowledgments

Grateful acknowledgment is made to the following publications in which most of these poems have appeared:

The American Scholar: *Comprehension*; Approach: *Questions Requiring No Answer, Time to Consider, Continued Story*; Audience: *The Turtle*; Beloit Poetry Journal: *Death by Tractor*; Bitterroot: *War Orphan*; The Chicago Tribune Magazine: *The Lighted Windows, The Magnet*; The Christian Science Monitor: *The Construction Crane, The Evidence, In the Willow's Shade, As in a Hiroshige*; Colorado Quarterly: *The Whippoorwill*; Defenders of Wildlife News: *Marsh*; The Educational Forum: *Still Life: Seventeenth Century Dutch, Moon Rock*; Epos: *Forecast Uncertain*; Harper's Bazaar: *Starling In The Snow*; Hawk and Whippoorwill: *This Nearer Ground*; Hudson Review, Vol. VIII, No. 2: *American Vineyard*; Impetus: *The Mask*; Imprints Quarterly: *Likenesses*; Japanophile: *Two Ch'an Scrolls*; The Lyric: *Mural at Teotihuacan*; The New York Times: *Red-tailed Hawk*; North Shore Magazine: *Coastal Fog*; Paintbrush: *Once I looked deep into the Trees*; Poet Lore: *Rescue at Noonday, Basswood Trees in Flower, Child Lost, Pictorial Message on Pioneer 10*; The Saturday Review of Literature: *Radio at Night*; South and West: *In a Dry Time, Mayan Story, Six Medals Given to Hero's Widow*; Spirit: *The Doves in the Eaves, Second Sight*; The Transatlantic Review: *Travelogue with Slides*; University of Kansas City Review: *The Emperor's Robe, Lost River, Death of a Fox*; The University Review: *Art of India: Dancing God (Bronze Figure)*; Virginia Quarterly Review: *The Egrets, Bailey's Pond*; Voices: *Abandoned Quarry, Black Angus and Black Crows*; Western Humanities Review: *Landscape with Figure, The Dancing Girls*; Wormwood Review: *Oh, There are Lovers Still*;

National Federation of State Poetry Societies' Anthology of Prize Poems: *In Time of Change*. *Questions Requiring No Answer* won the national Gwendolyn Brooks Award given by Approach. *Child Lost* received a Poet Lore annual award for 1971. *Study in Contrasts* won a New York Poetry Forum Award 1977 for a poem on ecology.

6

Introduction

THOUGH several hundred of her poems have been published in a wide variety of journals over many years, *Time to Consider* is, remarkably, Mildred Cousens' first book. At eighty-five she has (in all senses) had time to consider, to consider how her life is rooted in a world where "consider" still derives from the Latin sense of observing a star group to tell time or to locate one's self.

In poem after poem, Mildred Cousens locates herself by how carefully she observes the nature of this planet. She is an exacting skeptic ("If I had not seen, I would not believe . . ."), but she is open to every aspect of what she sees. Considering how a turtle "crossed our afternoon," she recognizes that

> He will be living years from now,
> persistent, antediluvian, dumb,
> in lonely marshes of the mind,
> however wise we may become.

Asking herself in a different "Marsh" why she is so "uneasy," she comes to understand that in just such "essential slime / the dance of cells began, / . . . / newt, snail and mammal, / source of men and marvels, / myths, dreams, and time."

Such close-in seeing and far ranging speculation are hallmarks of Mildred Cousens' work. "Patience, hope, persistence" (indeed, her considerable virtues) incline her not only to define the nature of her own lifetime, but to project her imagination deeply into the past and courageously into the future. Examining an exhibition "Moon Rock," she sees it before her "as dangerous, as wonderful / as that first forbidden apple." Just as considerable time here extends from her own lifetime to moon rock to Eden, so is she fully capable

7

of returning her poems from marsh and moonscape to surviving immediate pain and ongoing grief.

Having lost both son and husband, Mildred Cousens knows what it is to walk a "de Chirico landscape / block after block. . . ." She can admit to knowing "not I, but my world is dying." Yet both within and beyond such trauma and prognosis, she has the resilience to recognize "Oh, there are lovers still" in the shadows of an island's new oiltanks, and to permit herself the marginal realization that she, too, "may live again / in the world warmed by sun, / hands, words, and love."

What lovely luck it is to have in hand this book by a woman who, born just six months after the Wright brothers flew, still yearns to involve her own words with a "Pictorial Message . . ." rocketed into space. In how she has both held to old ways and responded to new, Mildred Cousens is a remarkable member of a remarkable generation of women: women whose lives, *lifelong,* have been assaulted and embraced by exponential change. *Time to Consider* defines a life caringly lived, generously written, by a woman who has the courage and intelligence to ask

> What is it we have nearly forgotten?
> What is it we almost know?

"However wise we may become" is still an open question, but if we can be as open to reading Mildred Cousens' poems as she has been in writing them, we are surely bound to be wiser.

PHILIP BOOTH

May, 1989

8

Contents

IV

V

VI

I

For a Human Reason

The Egrets

Three white egrets stood in the morning marsh,
motionless as figures stenciled upon glass,
their stemlike legs deep in the chill black water,
beaks all pointing across the open landscape
beyond the murky water, the wild morass.

Three white egrets, scarcely believable,
pure as Platonic virtues though less rare,
still as if waiting for a sign or signal
till from the tall pine grove a fourth one flew,
wheeling and circling in the sunlit air

over the others till they came alive,
lifted their beaks, fan-spread their folded wings,
forsook at last the dark primeval water,
wheeled and circled, then following their leader,
soared and flew in ever lessening rings
toward an unknown, yet somehow known horizon—

I called him courage for a human reason.

Bailey's Pond

Who Bailey was no one remembers
and nobody seems to know or care
who owns it now or the land about.
An Ice Age ago wide waters flowed
over these hills now nearly bone-bare,
save for the thickly wooded rim
of the deep tarn black as a well.
No visible stream flows out or in
yet hidden channels must lead to the river
some miles away, for they say the drowned
never return, are never found.

The summer we sought adventure there
under the spruce and tamaracks
out tents were intruders beneath the trees,
out laughter came back in mocking echoes
from opposite steeply sloping shores.
Round evening fires with lowered voice
some one told us the villagers' tales
of witches, werewolf, a murder unsolved.
By day we swam but never dared
beyond our depth lest we be lost.
Our red canoes were open wounds
on the dark surface of the pond.
Nights we lay in our hammocks and watched
the moon seductive, shimmering, pale
and slept to dream still under her spell.
The dawn came slowly, sunless, cold.
When we broke camp before we planned
we seemed ourselves milleniums old.

The Turtle

We lay among the maidenhair,
pillowed on myriad, feathery fronds
of new-sprung moss, and dreamed we held
the farthest future in our hands.

High in the tangled topmost boughs
sunlight glistened, as if through
Gothic windows, crystal, gold,
leaf-patterned green, celestial blue;

but when we saw some pines away
pale fingers beckoning through the gloom,
fungus flowers it seems they were,
we rose and left our peaceful room,

walking along the forest floor,
wary of sodden mould and damp—
and there an aged turtle was,
in the black ooze rimming the swamp.

With head and legs and tail outthrust,
his shell a fallen, darkened moon,
a mute reminder of time past,
he slowly crossed our afternoon.

He will be living years from now,
persistent, antediluvian, dumb,
in lonely marshes of the mind,
however wise we may become.

The Whippoorwill

Under the cottage lights we play the game,
skillfully fingering, flicking the glossy cards;
heads bent, eyes intent on the colorful antique symbols
until release, sigh, laughter, count and reshuffle;
talk of yesterday's picnic, tomorrow's plans;
then once more to the round with deal-again hope
as if this game, this moment of time were all—

Listen—from over the darkened water,
in the thousand trees out there
a questioning voice, a strange, insistent call—
   when oh where
   when oh where
Heads lift, turn as we look at each other,
hearing the wild cry from outside our circle,
beyond the thin pine walls, the bridge lamp's glow—
   when oh where
   when oh where
What is it we have nearly forgotten?
What is it we almost know?

Time to Consider

Below us curved the lake,
azure in sunlight, in cloud shadow jade,
a long narrow oval bound by gradual hills,
their treed sides showing a tinge of yellow-green,
the farther gullies dark with hemlock, pine.

We left our coats and trappings in the car,
sought out the path leading to the ravine
down past the towhee's constant questioning
in the old farm orchard, forsaken, overgrown,
where we could hear a brook now newly freed
rushing over boulders and logs in waterfalls.

Among damp leaves and ferns still tight as scrolls
we came on rose-hued fringed polygala
too rare to pick. We found white trilliums
but left them there among the ancient stones—
some other pair might need their lanterns too—
then followed the winding stream in search of fossils.

The sun was setting as we climbed the slope,
leaving behind our winter-weariness,
bearing a handful of pebbles, a seaworm's trace,
a crinoid mold, a shell intaglio,
with a seedling oak, its roots still cradled in moss.

American Vineyard

This is an ancient pattern on these hills—
the lines of silvery stakes
climb up the contoured rows of terraces;
the unseen shuttle of the sun
has woven them all about with leaves
guarding the ripening clusters with their green.

Some patterns are erased by time and place;
others are dimmed, remaining echoes only—
the pomegranate, bird of paradise,
the lotus blossom and the Persian pear
survive on clay or wood, parchment and tapestry.

This one withstands
the stormy rigors of a harsher land.
It once knew Canaan and Assyria,
and then the isles of Cyprus and of Crete,
Provence and Andalusia, Tuscany—
Remember? You have even heard it named
within the rhythms of the Odyssey—
the gardens of Alcinöus, the sea as dark as wine—
think how the strand weaves through the web of years,
a many tendrilled vine.

Questions Requiring No Answer

Directly stated, the evolution of the entire
universe—stars, elements, life, man—is a
process of drawing something out of nothing,
out of the utter void of non-being. . .
    —Loren Eiseley, *The Mind as Nature*

How can I think of nowhere
when my mind is filled with Andes,
Egypt, prairies, rivers,
oceans, moon, and stars;
or how imagine nothing
when my inner eye sees always
maple, oak, and linden
in leaf or winter bare,
tall grass waving in summer,
blue lupin by the roadside,
farmyard cock and cattle,
wood thrush, fallow deer?

How can I conceive
of a dark and shoreless void
as source of all our suns,
atom and galaxy,
and that same energy
whereby I think and dream
and feel and speak and move?

Comprehension

Down the dim lit corridors
of labyrinthian mind,
slowly moves the silent thought,
careful as the blind

who know with sure decisive hands
the way solution lies
though deep amorphous shadow rests
upon their empty eyes.

Abandoned Quarry

This massive man-made cliff,
this brownstone bluff
once echoed with the rough
sound of metal on shale,
the screech of saw and drill.

Look over the edge
where it drops through time
sheer to the black-green water,
there by that deepest ledge
you can gauge the measure of men's labor.
The century it took to cut this pit
down through Triassic rock
is less than a second by earth's clock.

Now beside the rim
these great blank monoliths remain,
standing in silent multitudes,
or lying like fallen gods
among the sorrel and the dry burdock.
The curious mark upon that broken block
is the fossil footprint of a dinosaur—
look long and you may elude the mesh
the known years make and turn
and follow the track through giant ferns
to a vanished shore.

This Nearer Ground

The glacier must have carved this gorge:
a torrent swirling
gouged ancient rock to form a deep ravine,
now overhung with fringe of evergreen,
while underfoot
pale moss and dusky mold
line the path along the precipice.
See there below the quiet stream,
all that is left of a once raging river,
threading the shadowy glen with silver.

There is no way across,
no way into that distant wood,
unless you travel miles around,
no matter how much you may wish
to know the story that the past discloses.
But look upon this nearer ground,
here in the fallen leaves
a sodden scarf with faded red silk roses.

II

The Artist-Seer

Museum: Chinese Wing

I
THE EMPEROR'S ROBE

Four centuries old this rare brocaded gown,
with sleeves outspread and pinned against the wall,
a five-clawed dragon coiled upon its breast,
and the sun a ruby ball

centered in shining rays of golden thread.
An octagon turtle crawls over azure silk
while gay embroidered bats at noonday fly
through clouds like curds of milk.

Mulberry leaves are green in a nameless season.
They mingle with flowering sprays of quince and plum,
and a phoenix arises from ashes, the dying embers
a wilted chrysanthemum.

We examine the handwork, admiring the infinite skill,
the patience of minions, the culture of ancient Honan—
then what, we inquire, of the high Son of Heaven himself?
But no one can tell of the man.

II
LANDSCAPE WITH FIGURE

Tall mountains climb the paper tier on tier,
white puffs of mist define the altitude;
a shaded pathway winds beneath a sheer
pine-bristled cliff, while tufts of delicate-hued

flowers peer round rocks of blackest ink—
and there a hardy, ageless traveler
whose chief vocation seems to be to think
journeys alone, a mute philosopher.

His passive brow, his calm, unwrinkled cheeks,
his eyes remote, his lean and quiet hands
reveal no hint of the far goal he seeks—
yet though his face, inscrutable, withstands

our curious wonder and our questioning,
we know that he has crossed the bridge of doubt
over that torrent wildly eddying—
and is quite certain what he is about.

III

THE DANCING GIRLS
Figurines—T'ang Dynasty

Grave robbers or archaeologists
rescued these maidens from a narrow room.
Though still confined, they smile behind the glass,
no more perhaps than in the royal tomb.

Now in a truce with time these three have gained
reprieve from darkness and oblivion.
The careful light discloses on the clay
traces of pigment, jade, vermilion

where graceful garments flow in lotus lines,
symbol of life, renascent and immortal;
their white arms seem to move before our eyes
in the strange rhythms of a ritual—

they must be weary and wish the hidden lute
would cease its endless music. Yet they keep
their poses for our pleasure, as they tried
to cheer their prince who much preferred to sleep.

IV

STARLING IN THE SNOW

With drooping wings, bowed head and lowered beak,
he stands huddled as though at last bereft
even of hope, his barbed feet clutching the bleak
edge of the icy drift.

He has no urge for flight, the winter skies
are hostile country, yet on the frozen ground
the vine is stripped of berries. There too his eyes
see only alien land.

Mu Ch'i, the painter, observing his distress
and pitying all creatures everywhere
forlorn, lost in a world's cold emptiness,
depicted his despair;

but he was wise as well as compassionate—
for there, high over the bird and his grave need
he drew a down-curved branch to counter fate,
with a cone, the living seed.

Exhibition: Art of India
DANCING GOD—BRONZE FIGURE

within the flaming circle
of time's endless riddle
four-armed, darkly smiling,
braceleted and bangled,
Siva, destroyer, dancer,
slays the fierce-toothed tiger
with his little finger;
breaks the back of the serpent,
flings it around his shoulder
slack as a flower garland;
stamps on a dwarfed mis-shapen
grovelling human figure;
vanquishes all evil,
wrong and woe and rancor,
within the living circle
of earth's timeless riddle,
Siva, destroyer, dancer,
tireless one, transformer

Two Ch'an Scrolls
FROM ZEN TEMPLE, DAITSOKUJI

What can they know
in that Northern land
of fiery dragon
or jungle tiger?

No matter that one
is legendary,
the other far
in another country,

it is enough
the artist-seer
knows himself,
is aware
of passion, rage,
the fangs of fear.

With brushstrokes sure
yet light as laughter
on these silk panels
he is master
of deep desire
and primal terror.

Mayan Story

They challenge men,
the cryptic markings
carved skillfully on stone,
these hieroglyphs
on blocks of granite hewn
from long-forgotten cities
buried in jungle growth, defying
linguist and scholar
who labor to decipher
their arcane story
and the mystery of their dying.

We too, curious, study
lintel, stele, altar,
trace the symbols pictured;
zigzag lightning, spike-rayed sun;
jaguar leaping, serpent coiled;
tasseled maize, proud-plumed bird.
We recognize the inscrutable One,
the god of rain,
above the hollowed basin
dark with an ancient stain,
nor do we need the word
to read the human faces,
masks of frenzy, fear, rage;
this one smiling, serene;
that one indomitable, strong—
they speak a language
that needs no tongue.

Mural at Teotihuacan

Butterflies blown by the wind
over the mountains
from the Eastern sea,
rain-sign of Quetzalcoatl,
once friendly deity,
seem still clinging
to this rose-hued palace wall.

An ancient artisan
incised each fragile wing,
the delicate antennae,
as if he wrought a jewel
of intricate design.
Men move as in a maze
among the butterflies,
dancing, swaying, singing,
praying in their need
for rain, rain, rain,
rain for the root and seed,
rain for the stunted grain,
rain for the dying valley.

Crumbling stone,
deserted temple,
fallen gods here testify
that Quetzalcoatl finally
must have passed them by.

Still Life
SEVENTEENTH CENTURY DUTCH

Chased candlestick, urn of silver,
cool smoothness of metal
against the woven roughness
of a warm red Persian carpet;
two full-blown roses lying
on shadowy folds of velvet;
Venetian wine glass holding
shimmer of liquid gold;
an orange cut, revealing
wheelspokes, the peel a spiral;
pale grapes near bursting
their skin's misted ovals;
a pyramid of peaches
glowing in a bowl.

Here human handiwork
is eloquent on canvas,
and fruits and flowers
are offered us to savor,
with form, color, light,
and one man's love of living
thrusting back the darkness
of three hundred years.

III

An Unfinished Scroll

Continued Story

We wake this morning
to a winter landscape,
snow white as parchment
with tree branches, twigs
in intricate tracery
punctuated here and there by birds,
commas, periods, a pair of quotation marks,
all still as if the tale were ended.

The light increasing
there begins again
the movement of cars and people,
first slow, then hurried,
with clusters of children
in red hood, blue cap, green jacket,
like colored illustrations
along the newly lettered lines.

I try to read, but cannot quite translate
this living chronicle,
this ancient Sanskrit,
its sources half-forgotten,
still being written on an unfinished scroll.

The Construction Crane

A long Jacob's ladder,
it reaches skyward
above the busy street,
by day its black iron framework
stark and ominous.
From time to time it swings,
steel wires and pulleys swaying,
moved by an unseen hand.
A giant hook lowers a heavy beam,
settles it gently into place;
lifts a metal hod
filled with wet concrete
to an upper level,
while out of the loud confusion
of rolling mixers, trucks in gear,
clanging shovels, hammering, yells,
the building slowly rises
floor by floor.

Late afternoon a whistle sounds,
releasing pandemonium,
then all is still,
the tall structure motionless
until another morning.

Now in the evening,
though we can see no angels
ascending or descending,
its topmost rung leans
against a dark blue heaven,
and a quarter moon,
a shining golden bucket,
is hanging in its chains.

Rescue at Noonday

High over the city street he hung
as on a medieval gibbet,
his arm caught by an iron girder
fallen slantwise across a lurching beam.
Firetruck and ladder had come to his aid,
workmen hurried with flaming torch
and tools of their trade to save him,
their own lives dangling
from that narrow perch.

Bankers, brokers, shoppers, clerks,
taximan, newsboy, a woman in mink
stood looking upward appalled that a man
a moment ago master of his calling,
sure-footed a hundred feet in air,
should be now a helpless thing.

For that long hour we were as one,
watching, waiting—
until a loud clang of metal, a crash of timber
turned us to stone.
When the dust cleared
and we saw him, face torture pale, but safe,
the crowd gasped with relief,
then clapped and cheered those
sweat-stained, helmeted heroes.

The Mask

Sleek as a leopard, coat of leopard skin,
pale blond, bepearled, and oh so elegant
in her demeanor, at first insouciant
she views the mask—the geometric grin,
the arched and sneering nostrils deep inlaid
with pierced gold glittering on the ebony,
the slits for eyes narrowed inscrutably,
the brow and chin gashed as though scarified.

Helpless she stands before the hypnotic stare
with writhing roots around her, a dark swamp
dragging her downward till the jungle damp
invades her flesh and a long-forgotten fear
tenses her fingers, as alone and lost,
she clutches the rim of the primeval past.

Death by Tractor

Spring greens the land,
transformed by sun
the waiting trees now rise
in sprays of scintillant green.

Across the new-ploughed field
dark furrows lead the way
to the steep slope curving round the boulder
where half hidden by the clumsy beast
failed in its maneuver
and fallen on its side,
the engine churning, churning,
a crumpled figure lies
face down in morning dew
like a bound sack tossed from a load
or a wind-ruined scarecrow prone.

He does not hear
the red-winged blackbirds
singing in the clump of alders,
nor does he care
that quail are nesting
among his winter wheat,
nor notice at the farmhouse window
the white face, frozen in disbelief,
trying not to understand
that he has made so soon his final payment
on these, his own few acres,
his earned land.

Child Lost

Child, daughter,
wherever you are,
in a strange city, in a strange house
of dark hallways, dingy rooms,
a place of no love, no light,
captive alone
or surrounded by faces
hostile, mad, obscene,
in your young innocence fearing the unknown,
or worse, your faith now broken,
may you remember always before you sleep
how we said goodnight, dear one, goodnight.

If it should be at a field's edge
with milkweed pods and asters,
where late dewberries black as spiders' eyes
watch from their webs of briars,
or if it should be in the woodlands
where you might have wandered,
on the forest floor woven with pine needles,
fallen cones, mosses, fern,
where oak leaves rustle above you like blown paper,
we know you would not be afraid—
but oh, my child,
you may be cold and hungry,
you may be scratched, bruised, wounded
by thorns, stones, or men—
and if while you are sleeping, the ants and beetles dare—
then, now it is nearly winter,
may the snow fall gently on you
and cover you with a soft white blanket
and shield you until we come.

War Orphan

Today I have seen the face of hunger,
eyesockets hollow, eyes staring;
grooved ribcage, distorted limbs
whose shrunken muscles have forgotten motion,
the blood no longer cares.

I have seen the oval shell
that houses that most delicate machine, the brain,
toppling on the neck
like a heavy seedpod on a broken stem.
The mask of flesh drawn tight over cheek and jaw
cannot conceal
that final image common to us all.

A stranger to love, to joy,
this small child may die
believing life is hunger.

The Lighted Windows

Sometimes in the evening
I watch the lighted windows
appear in shining rectangles
one by one or in rows,
a nightly panorama
up the neighboring hillside;

veiled by springtime foliage
waving in the wind,
or by strands of rain;
in winter arced by treelimbs,
the golden panes segmented,
outlined like stained glass.

High on the horizon
chains of white light gleam,
a hall, a laboratory.
Where houses were an amber
or Mondrian-yellow square
may shield a grief or joy.

Slowly the numbers lessen.
Past midnight only a few
mark the familiar contours,
a dimly shaded one,
a scholar working late,
a child in need of care.

Hour by hour they change,
vary with the season
and the passing years,
soon or late in turn,
one by one or in rows,
to vanish in the dark.

Radio at Night

Now is the time that the dark flows in
    from the wide Atlantic—
the edge of the shadow glides over the miles of land,
covering the restless continent far to its western beaches
with the peace of the homecoming hour and the
    stillness of night.

Then over the hemisphere listening there in the darkness
the voices, the many voices hover like birds in the air
that dip to earthward and rising, flutter and disappear.

The threads are tangled, the threads of sound, the golden
    music,
but over the lighted cities and towns where men are waiting
the words come clear as the clangor of bells.

The magic sound drifts over the Appalachian ridges—
over the broad lakes held in the cupped hands of the hills,
over the mighty rivers rushing along their valleys—
out in the far Dakotas the tired man hitches his rocker
across the faded carpet close to the dial—

Then lost, lost in the snows of the Rockies the voices,
like ice-clad planes they are lost—only the strains of music,
Schubert and Strauss and the wraiths of the women dancing
swirl in the storm on the mountain-peaks of the Rockies—

There on the coasts where all day long the sunlight glistened
the dark lies now, and the voices drift out over
the pale white crescents that gleam like thin young moons—

the songs and the dances, the news of the day and the speeches,
the voice of the suave announcer, the sound of the gong—
twelve o'clock by Pacific time—back in New York
the music is thinning a little, but in San Francisco
the fun is beginning, the wine just starting to flow.

The voices float out over the western ocean
and are lost like birds in the deep fog of the dark.

IV

Against the Time's Confusion

The Magnet

If I had not seen, I would not believe all they told me
of the thousands of wild geese that come in the early spring
to the marsh-rimmed pond not many miles out
    from the village—

They drift on the open water in feathered flotillas,
their heads and necks S-curved like antique prows.
They rise from the water with a spreading of massive wings,
a sudden opening of gray-brown shutters,
closing again as they settle back on the surface,
their feet upended before them to brake their flight.
In late afternoon they fly in lesser squadrons
to the leeward shore to feed in last year's stubble
or to rest for the night in the dried marsh grass or shallows.
There they talk and they talk, how they gabble and gossip
in loud language, a continual conversation,
each by itself a clown with a clumsy body,
yet together their movements a study in order and grace.

If we should return almost any day now,
they might have already begun
their long journey north to breeding grounds in the Arctic,
in serried formation like so many iron filings,
as if they were somehow drawn,
and then we might search the sky, shore, marshes, and
    wide pond water
and find not one.

Marsh

In this secluded marsh
cattails in clusters rise
among thick-tufted reeds,
brown velvet pinnacles
above the muck and ooze,
perches for singing blackbirds,
goldfinches, dragonflies
until the summer sun
gives way to autumn chill.
Like burnt-out torches then
they slant across the pools,
refuge for merganser,
mallard, blue-winged teal.

But why am I uneasy—
we seem so alien here
in this diminished land
of life in miniature,
yet this film of algae,
this green pond scum
is a place of happenings,
of hidden chemistry
and ancient origins.
In such essential slime
the dance of cells began,
amoeba, protozoa,
newt, snail, and mammal,
source of men and marvels,
myths, dreams, and time.

In the Willow's Shade

I stand on the old stone bridge
and watch the water
flowing in silent ripples
beneath the arch.
There willow leaves float,
a school of silver minnows—
strangely they do not vanish
when I move.

As in a Hiroshige

the cherry trees in bloom in this spring landscape
are rose-tinted acres islanded in green,
the trunks and twisted branches of the orchard
ink-dark brush strokes against the tawny soil,
and there in the corner three blackbirds settled down,
the artist's signature.

The Doves in the Eaves

Today the doves
are moaning in the eaves.
It cannot be from hunger,
for there are seeds and crumbs,
surely food enough
for taking on the ground.
They do not lack for shelter,
nor can it be
that they are lonely,
they have each other.

Over and over they repeat
the sound of grieving.
Perhaps they sense
the coming cold,
though now the sun is warm,
the sky is clear,
as sometimes
in the midst of happiness
we know an inner sadness,
a secret fear
of future loss.

Second Sight

How can I paint these peaches in a bowl?
I have no canvas, brushes, pigments even,
but I would conjure up with syllables
the amber glass holding in its curve
these glowing spheres, saffron shading to coral;
and then their texture,
softer than suede, or a young boy's cheek—
yet as I write I know I can do more
than paint them as they are,
for I have second sight:

I see them now cut open
though still intact here on my table,
two golden halves, one set with a giant ruby,
the fragrant juice oozing out like honey
for someone, who knows when or where,
reading these words, to savor.

Likenesses

The flowering dogwood
is a young dancer,
a ballerina
on springtime grass;
deep in the summer
a flowing fountain
in rain or sunlight
glittering green;
berries ripened,
a flaming crimson,
the flare of a match
in the autumn wind;
through the long winter
the stripped branches
thin ribs of silver,
a skeleton.

Turning seasons
repeat the cycle:
woman, water,
burning, bone.

Red-Tailed Hawk

Just then from nowhere a great wild hawk
swooped in a long diminishing arc
down over the bone-bleached stubble,
feathers mottled light and dark,
tyrant head, steel-bright beak,
outstretched talons bent on evil.

I saw him land, sure as an arrow,
his tail spread wide
in a red imperial train,
but I knew terror, pain;
I was the paralyzed mouse,
the mangled sparrow.

Black Angus and Black Crows

Along this country road
I am amazed to see
Black Angus in a field
fertile with sunlit gold.

Nebulous after-image
or shadowed negative?
But I am not deceived,
the creatures live and move.

In long black shaggy coats,
tams and kilts and socks,
heifers as well as steers,
they graze among the shocks.

These beasts of moor and glen,
dark tarn and burn and fen
were bred on oats and barley,
not in this landscape surely.

Black crows fly overhead.
With ragged wings they paint
scrawls upon the sky
of scurrilous complaint,

reviling, screeching scorn
against these alien Celts
with their outlandish pelts
among the native corn.

Death of a Fox

A red-gold flame, the old fox must be dying
under these teasels and timothy gone to seed.
Gray smoke drifts from the burst pods of milkweed
above him where he is lying.

Once he was rather a respected creature,
a little the rake, but a gentleman of sorts,
valued even by kings for his skill in sports,
renowned for his subtle nature.

Fools and fowls feared him and many a fable
made him a hero or at least a protagonist.
Though hounded by critic and baited by satirist,
they recognized he was able.

Reynard they called him. He was held in high esteem
by Aesop, Geoffrey Chaucer, and La Fontaine
who made him immortal, if at times a villain—
see how his eyes still gleam.

The Evidence

Early morning light on the leaves,
shining green shields of maples,
silver spear-points of elm,
dark bristle-brushes of pine,

wake me to new assurance,
as forms, variations, resemblances
voice their affirmation
against the time's confusion.

Remembering last winter's storm,
the wind's mad violence,
the crushing burden of ice
that broke the weaker boughs,

I marvel at these trees
nourished by melted snows,
roots thrusting deeper in the ground
while sap fountains up through the bole,

even to the outermost branch,
to feed a richer foliage,
as if in answer to life's need
to keep a steady balance.

V

On a Secret, Lonely Voyage

Lost River

Between tall cattails and green arrowhead,
the gold marsh lilies parting at our bow,
we rowed upriver in the morning sun.
Toy turtles startled by our dripping oars
slipped from their island logs. Blue dragonflies
zigzagged around as we moved slowly on
until we reached the sheltered shallow place
beneath a willow, then let our anchor slide
down through the water clearer than any glass.

The light flowed back in liquid bubbling rays
from glittering sand, each stone a sculptured thing
in that new element as fine as air.
Half-proud of our own cunning and deceit,
we watched the pale perch nibbling at our lines.
Half-shamed, half-glad we drew them struggling in,
half-sad we watched their opalescence die,
So died our innocence each added year.

I have come back and cannot even find
what then I knew, only a shrunken stream
flowing through ragged weedstalks, and that once
rush-fringed, sun-flecked, still remembered river
darkened with waste and the debris of time.

Oh, There Are Lovers Still

Centuries old the willows on that island,
a half-moon lying within the river bend,
carved by the glacier or an ancient flood.
Winters revealed gray knotted trunks and branches
woven with withes, interlaced with vines,
but in another season the warm rains
fostered a jungle, a mysterious wood.
"Remember, never land there," we were warned
lest we encounter danger, who knew what
poisonous fangs, what quicksand or quagmire?

And so by day, youth-curious, we rowed
close to the weedy bank, where we could see,
peering into the leafy emerald twilight,
the long-toothed brakes crouched on the island floor,
wild orchises, sometimes a cardinal flower
burning as if to tempt us further in.
On summer nights, safe-anchored in a cove,
we watched the silver serpent of the current
and talked of life, our future, the unknown
in quiet voices, the only other sound
the ripples gently lapping at our prow.

Now all the trees are down, the island bare,
a bridge built over, a grove of chimney stacks
where once we yearned but did not dare to trespass.
Black barges nudge the roughhewn timber pier,
oil tanks rise in rows along the shore.
The moonlight shines on oil-slick darkened waters.
Oh, there are lovers still, in the long shadow
of the mammoth aluminum-painted cylinders.

In a Dry Time

All that month long we waited for the rain,
seeing the grasses bleach to brittle straw,
the young leaves drop one by one from the bough,
the tentative fruit shrivel on tree and vine;
each quick stream narrowed to a sluggish snake
crawling among stones; the shrunken lake
revealing honeycombed clay or slimy mud
where only rank weeds flourished and grew tall.

We searched the hot sky shiny as new tin
for the occasional cloud, the thunderhead
seeming to promise change, relief, and yet
they did not let their hoarded waters fall—
while I who had mocked at magic was amazed
to hear myself from some deep well within
repeating, imploring before it was too late,
"Send oh send the healing waters down,"
my lips affirming what my mind refused.

Basswood Trees in Flower

This night in early summer
we lie with windows wide
and breathe the honey fragrance
of basswood trees in flower.
The curtains drift like foam
on invisible waves of air,
Overhead we hear a plane.

We do not envy them,
the far sky travelers
who fly above the clouds
companioned by the stars;
but now a siren sound,
reminder of fear and pain,
disturbs the scented dark.
Come closer, love, again.

The clock ticks on and on,
yet for this little while
it is enough to lie
unquestioning, satisfied
to be ourselves a part
of the earth's secret scheme—
and so we turn to sleep—
morning will bring the bees
here to this street, our world
under the blossoming trees

Coastal Fog

Today the islands float
almost invisible
behind a screen of gauze,
scattered fragments
on a sea with no horizon.

Here and there
dark fir pinnacles
emerge from the still whiteness.
We trace the contours,
remembering maps we have known.

Out on the reef
a fog horn calls its constant warning.
Nearer a bell-buoy clangs
to mark the channel
for the lost one, the boat astray

as in a dream
far from a familiar harbor
one sails strange waters,
past hidden shoals and misty headlands
on a secret, lonely voyage.

Trauma

I walked in a lonely de Chirico landscape
block after block on a street going far
no one came toward me   nobody passed me
nor was there any sound

walls without windows rose beside me
I could not find a welcoming door
signs were all in a foreign language
in that timeless city

Though the air around me was glaring sunlight
strange black shadows loomed here and there
as with weighted steps I moved along
on the hard stone pavement

I could not go back   I could not run
I had no choice but to travel on
until I would reach that certain brink
the final edge of darkness

and then I woke to the world of people
birds   animals
trees   grass   and flowers
someone was calling my name

Prognosis

"Grief never kills one,"
the doctor said,
as I recounted my symptoms,
"Get plenty of rest,
do not try not to weep,
walk out in the fresh air,
you will recover in time."
I could not believe him,
so sharp, so deep the pain.

When I looked in the mirror
I saw a stranger,
When I stared from the window
the landscape was grayed,
leaves all faded,
flowers funereal.
At last when I ventured
out among people
their faces were phantoms,
their voices diminished.

Yet I could still see and hear,
my limbs could move
though I ached in mind and body.
Then I knew he was right,
not I, but my world was dying.

Loss

Deep grief
dark cavern
no light   no air
and I prone
on the cold floor.

Fierce pain
dull ache
penetrate flesh and bone
all my senses numb
except for the vital wound,

nor can I reason
or think of the future
in this prison of despair
where day and night
are as one—

yet now a glimmer,
a faint flicker within
tells me I may live again
in the world warmed by sun,
hands, words, and love.

Once I Looked Deep into the Trees

Once I looked deep into the trees,
seeing the leaves
with all their variations.

For a long time I studied
their random flutterings,
how they changed in the changing light.

I looked deep into the boughs
where the green receded into darkness,
where the outline of each leaf was lost,

remembering that finally
generation after generation
would fall in a last glowing.

I looked deep into the trees,
considering sun, rain, soil, seed,
the repetition of the cycle,

yet could not find the reason
either for their being or their loss—
now I am contented with the leaves.

VI

On a Small World

Travelogue with Slides

Over the Hanging Gardens now the dust
lies like an old burnoose.
Beyond the broken walls stretch miles of sand.
Note how the lens focussed
on these crumbling yellow bricks
reveals a few ancient relics.
Here are some closer views
of sculptured animals,
lions, eagles, bulls,
headless or half worn away,
the tiles of colored clay
that clothed them then long since dissolved—
three thousand times or more has Babylon
revolved around the sun.

Belshazzar was a name to conjure with—
men fell on their faces when he spoke.
The Medes or was it Persians brought him down?
Close by his palace
a goatherd in a coarse black cloak
watches his hungry flock.
The Gate of Ishtar is fallen,
despoiled by the god of war.

See here above the tombs
a vulture soars
and there are nights the wild hyena roams
the roofless corridors.
The world is still within these photographs,
but in the ruins the hyena laughs.

Six Medals Given to Hero's Widow
—*Headline*

Summoned to this occasion
here in this hall of history,
I must not waver
nor give way to tears
at the sound of martial music.
For his children's sake
I must remember
to stand erect till the final notes
of the familiar anthem.
Such rituals are meant for the living,
to assuage our grief;
the dead have no need of ceremony.

His fellow countrymen pay their respects
with flags and symbols.
They say it also with flowers,
roses, carnations, white and crimson,
their scent heavy and sweet.

The high ones stand in line,
grave-countenanced, dignified.
Their words are kind,
they speak of honor, pride,
the ultimate sacrifice.

From their hands
I receive the ribboned medals,
hearing my voice from far-away repeating
the necessary memorized syllables.

I read the lauding inscriptions,
the loved name six times over,
Gently I touch the bronze, the silver—
they are cold.

Forecast Uncertain

The gray hills
huddle together on the horizon
like great humped beasts,
mastodons, mammoths
captive there in the distance,
or a herd of grazing bison
turned to stone in their tracks.

A rose-gold sunset
edges their backs with light,
outlines cloud continents,
islands afloat on
the sky's wide ocean;
gilds the rooftops, the windows
of houses across the valley;
illumines the trees' branches
where homing birds now gather.

If I had not read
the day's headlines,
nor heard the warning voices,
if I did not know
how swift the winds can rise
and with what violence,
if I were not aware
of the darkness deep in ourselves,
I would say, "It will be fair tomorrow."

Study in Contrasts

Every morning
the gulls fly inland,
headed for the city dump,
acres of refuse mounded
between the rusted railroad spur
and the new superhighway,
their long flight repeating
in rhythmic pattern
the ballet of the ocean,
spread wings white crests
on windblown waves.

As soon as the sky
is pearled with dawnlight
they forsake their watery home
and come down scavenging
among the sodden cartons,
empty cans, and broken glass,
seeming to prefer mouldy fragments,
easily-gotten offal
to the bittersweet mussels,
shell-bound snails,
and quicksilver herring
of their mother sea.

Every evening they return
in clusters trailing like smoke
from the factory chimneys
to the offshore islands,
the rocks and sand-duned beaches
clean-washed by the flowing tide.

Moon Rock

This priceless handful,
dull gray, unimpressive
piece of another planet,
wayward sister or foreigner
from farther space,
I can now view
in its clear plastic case.

The experts say it contains
no significant trace
of any precious substance,
that it bears no evidence
of water, no sign of life.

Neither physicist, astronomer,
geologist or chemist,
I cannot speak their language,
yet in this rough jewel
set in prongs of earthly metal
I see as if by X-ray
patience, hope, persistence,
the driving need to know.
I see this lunar object
displayed here before me
as dangerous, as wonderful
as that first forbidden apple.

Pictorial Message on Pioneer 10

To you, out there
beyond our atmosphere,
past Mars and Jupiter
on some far distant planet
along the Milky Way—
we send this golden tablet
marked with signs and symbols
that you may read
if you have eyes to see
and can comprehend.

We two creatures, man, woman,
standing beside the outlined
upright disc antenna
are two parts of the same being.
We live on a small world
in orbit round our sun,
on the third globe here drawn,
the arrow showing the source
of this vehicle
as well as its planned course.

By our raised hand
with its opposable thumb
we send you friendly greeting.
We tell you also thereby
that we are doers, molders, builders.
Then too, we are discoverers.
By these circles and lines
that you may recognize

as the two states of the atom,
we say we have harnessed its power.

The rayed beams
pulsing in varied rhythms
from fourteen living stars
to our earth at center
are meant to indicate
the time of launching;
the long horizontal line
behind our figures
to show where we are
in this, our galaxy.

As you may guess,
we are ourselves driven
by an inner force,
restless, curious.
For all our achievements,
at times in the dark we are lonely.
We shall be listening
for some answering signal,
hoping you are of like mind
and will speak to us.

In Time of Change

So now we come to the turn
beneath the cliffs.
There is no going back.
Behind us a haze obscures
the land we knew,
though we have records.
Before us the shadow cast
by the granite walls
darkens the ground.
The wind is cold and never
ceases blowing. Beside us
the few thin pines are scarred
and twisted, their gray roots
clutch at the rock.
Hawks soar over,
yet they seem not to heed us.
What lies ahead we can
no more than guess—
whether our way is upward
through the canyon
or downward into a barren
dry terrain.

If we rest here awhile
we could plan together
and choose what we would save
of our gear and treasure
in the event our path
grows even harder
as we struggle on in search
of living green.